THE PURPOSE DRIVEN TEACHER

A Reflective Journal

Reflect, Evolve, Inspire

DEAN & LEIGH
PUBLISHING LLC

Copyright © 2022 Shawn Brown-Brumfield
Dean & Leigh Publishing, LLC

All rights reserved. In accordance with the U.S. Copyright Act of 1976, the scanning, uploading, and electronic sharing of any part of this book without the permission of the publisher constitute unlawful piracy and theft of the author's intellectual property. If you would like to use material from the book (other than review purposes), prior written permission must be obtained by contacting the publisher at dean.leighpublishing@gmail.com. Thank you for your support of the author's rights.

Requests for information should be addressed to:
The Purpose-Driven Educator
Dean & Leigh Publishing, LLC
1443 E. Washington Blvd. #235
Pasadena, CA 91104

Dean.leighpublishing@gmail.com
www.thepurposedrivenschool.com

First Edition: January 2022

Dean & Leigh Publishing, LLC are trademarks

ISBN: 978-1-7377058-5-7
ISBN (hardcover): 978-1-7377058-6-4

Printed in the United State of America

This Journal Belongs to:

_____

DATES

Start:

_____

End:

_____

The Purpose-Driven Teacher
Reflect, Evolve, Inspire

Teachers are angels on earth. They have been afforded the highest level of responsibility given to mankind. They transform the minds and lives of students through the work that they do. Teachers provide a service that supports every profession. Their work significantly impacts students who then go on to work, serve, and lead in a variety of vocations, creating a ripple effect of positive change that extends to the rest of society.

In order for teachers to be effective, they must stay relevant and keep pace with the ever-so-changing times. That requires them to forever be students of the profession. As consummate students, teachers must endeavor to grow professionally, and real professional growth relies heavily on personal growth. It will be through self-awareness and an expansive perspective that professional development will have the biggest impact. How teachers grow as individuals will dictate the impact they have on students and those they encounter.

This journal is designed to help teachers Reflect, Evolve, and Inspire. Documenting one's own experiences, feelings, and "aha moments" will help to maximize personal and professional growth. As a teacher when you elevate to your highest self, you will have greater influence on students and, ultimately, humanity.

You are a light for your students, parents, and colleagues. Your influence lasts a life time.

Continue to learn and grow, fighting the good fight for the greater good of humanity!

"Education is not the filling of a pot but the lighting of a fire."
—W.B. Yeats

"Teaching is not a lost art, but the regard for it is a lost tradition"
-Jacques Barzun

"A teacher is one who makes himself progressively unnecessary."
-Thomas Carruthers

"I am not a teacher, but an awakener."

–Robert Frost

"I never teach my pupils; I only attempt to provide the conditions in which they can learn."

–Albert Einstein

"Teaching is the highest form of understanding."

—Aristotle

"When one teaches, two learn"

–Robert Heinlein

"A teacher affects eternity; he can never tell where his influence stops."
—Henry Adams

> "I cannot teach anybody anything, I can only make them think."
>
> —Socrates

"Those who know, do. Those that understand, teach."

—Aristotle

"I cannot be a teacher without exposing who I am"

−Paulo Freire

"In a completely rational society, the best of us would be teachers and the rest of us would have to settle for something else."

–Lee Iacocca

"The mediocre teacher tells. The good teacher explains. The superior teacher demonstrates. The great teacher inspires."

– William Arthur Ward

"The best teachers are the ones that change their minds."

—Terry Heick

"A good teacher is like a candle – it consumes itself to light the way for others."

–Mustafa Kemal Atatürk

> "A great teacher can teach Calculus with a paper clip and literature in an empty field. Technology is just another tool, not a destination."
> –Unknown

"Teaching is the one profession that creates all other professions."
-Unknown

"A teacher who is attempting to teach without inspiring the pupil with a desire to learn is hammering on cold iron."

—Horace Mann

"Good teaching is 1/4 preparation and 3/4 theatre."

–Gail Goldwin

"The job of an educator is to teach students to see vitality in themselves."
—Joseph Campbell

"Teachers have three loves: love of learning, love of learners, and the love of bringing the first two loves together."

–Scott Hayden

"You can teach a person all you know, but only experience will convince him that what you say is true."

–Richelle E. Goodrich

> "The greatest sign of success for a teacher is to be able to say, 'The children are now working as if I did not exist.'"
>
> –Maria Montessori

"Ask 'How will they learn best?' not 'Can they learn?'"

-Jaime Escalante

"It is essential to understand that battles are primarily won in the heart...(people) respond to leadership in a most remarkable way and once you have won (their) heart, (they) will follow you anywhere."

-Vince Lombardi

"It takes a big heart to help shape little minds."

-Unknown

"Far and away the best prize that life offers is the chance to work hard at work worth doing."

−Theodore Roosevelt

"It is the supreme art of the teacher to awaken joy in creative expression and knowledge."

-Albert Einstein

"If a child can't learn the way we teach, maybe we should teach the way they learn"

—Ignacio 'Nacho' Estrada

"The meaning of life is to find your gift. The purpose of life is to give it away."

–Pablo Picasso

"Teachers ask questions and help students find answers. Yet learning isn't only about finding the right answer, but also creating the road that leads to the answer. Learning with every step is the true sign of progress."

-Unknown

"Tell me and I forget. Teach me and I remember. Involve me and I learn."

–Benjamin Franklin

"Teaching is the greatest act of optimism"

–Colleen Wilcox

"In the face of disrespect, misbehavior, and lack of student enthusiasm, teachers are the believers. They see the light at the end of the tunnel and they lead step by step—truly the greatest act of optimism."

—Unknown

"If you are planning for a year, sow rice; if you are planning for a decade, plant trees; if you are planning for a lifetime, educate people."

–Chinese Proverb

"Education is not preparation for life; education is life itself."
—John Dewey

"What sculpture is to a block of marble, education is to a human soul"
-Joseph Addison

"Teaching is the one profession that creates all other professions."
—Unknown

"Education breeds confidence. Confidence breeds hope. Hope breeds peace."

—Confucius

"If someone is going down the wrong road, he doesn't need motivation to speed him up. What he needs is education to turn him around."

–Jim Rohn

"The dream begins, most of the time, with a teacher who believes in you, who tugs and pushes and leads you on to the next plateau, sometimes poking you with a sharp stick called truth." —Dan Rather

"The art of teaching is the art of assisting discovery."

–Mark Van Doren

"What the teacher is, is more important than what he teaches."

−Karl Meninger

"Every child deserves a champion—an adult who will never give up on them, who understands the power of connection and insists that they become the best that they can possibly be." —Rita Pierson

"Better than a thousand days of diligent study is one day with a great teacher."

—Japanese Proverb

"Teaching is more than imparting knowledge; it is inspiring change. Learning is more than absorbing facts; it is acquiring understanding."
-William Arthur Ward

"Children must be taught how to think, not what to think."

-Margaret Mead

"You can teach a student a lesson for a day, but if you can teach him to learn by creating curiosity, he will continue the learning process as long as he lives."
—Clay P. Bedford

"If kids come to us from strong, healthy, functioning families, it makes our job easier. If they do not come to us from strong, healthy, functioning families, it makes our job more important."

—Barbara Colorose

"What we want is to see the child in pursuit of knowledge, and not knowledge in pursuit of the child."

—George Bernard Shaw

"Students don't care how much you know until they know how much you care."

—Anonymous

> *"Education is the most powerful weapon which you can use to change the world."*
>
> —Nelson Mandela

"Every child should have a caring adult in their lives. And that's not always a biological parent or family member. It may be a friend or neighbor. Often times it is a teacher."

–Joe Manchin

"To this end the greatest asset of a school is the personality of the teacher."

–John Strachan

"Teach love, generosity, good manners and some of that will drift from the classroom to the home and who knows, the children will be educating the parents."
—Roger Moore

"A good teacher can inspire hope, ignite the imagination, and instill a love of learning."

−Brad Henry

"The art of teaching is the art of assisting discovery."

—Mark Van Doren

> "One good teacher in a lifetime may sometimes change a delinquent into a solid citizen."
>
> –Philip Wylie

"Failure is a great teacher, and I think when you make mistakes and you recover from them and you treat them as valuable learning experiences, then you've got something to share." —Steve Harvey

> "You never stop learning. If you have a teacher, you never stop being a student."
>
> –Elisabeth Rohm

"If you have to put someone on a pedestal, put teachers. They are society's heroes."

–Guy Kawasaki

"A good teacher is a determined person."

–Gilbert Highet

"None of us got where we are solely by pulling ourselves up by our bootstraps. We got here because somebody – a parent, a teacher, an Ivy League crony or a few nuns – bent down and helped us pick up our boots."

　　　　　　　　　　　　　　　　　　　　　　　　-Thurgood Marshall

> "I like a teacher who gives you something to take home to think about besides homework."
>
> –Lily Tomlin

"You have to grow from the inside out. None can teach you; none can make you spiritual. There is no other teacher but your own soul."

—Swami Vivekananda

"We discovered that education is not something which the teacher does, but that it is a natural process which develops spontaneously in the human being."
—Maria Montessori

"Those who know how to think need no teachers."
—Mahatma Gandhi

"The world of knowledge takes a crazy turn when teachers themselves are taught to learn."

-Bertolt Brecht

"The true aim of everyone who aspires to be a teacher should be, not to impart his own opinions, but to kindle minds."

–Frederick William Robertson

"A teacher affects eternity; he can never tell where his influence stops."
-Henry Adams

"A good teacher, like a good entertainer first must hold his audience's attention, then he can teach his lesson."
—John Henrik Clarke

"I was lucky that I met the right mentors and teachers at the right moment."

–James Levine

"The dream begins with a teacher who believes in you, who tugs and pushes and leads you to the next plateau, sometimes poking you with a sharp stick called 'truth.'" —Dan Rather

"One looks back with appreciation to the brilliant teachers, but with gratitude to those who touched our human feelings. The curriculum is so much necessary raw material, but warmth is the vital element for the growing plant and for the soul of the child." —Carl Jung

"Teachers can change lives with just the right mix of chalk and challenges."

–Joyce Meyer

"Good teachers know how to bring out the best in students."
—Charles Kuralt

"Most of us end up with no more than five or six people who remember us. Teachers have thousands of people who remember them for the rest of their lives."

-Andy Rooney

"The most important part of teaching is to teach what it is to know."
—Simone Weil

"The best teacher is the one who suggests rather than dogmatizes, and inspires his listener with the wish to teach himself."
—Edward G. Bulwer-Lytton

"The teacher is the one who gets the most out of the lessons, and the true teacher is the learner."

–Elbert Hubbard

"A professor is someone who talks in someone else's sleep."
— W. H. Auden

"Education is the key to success in life, and teachers make a lasting impact in the lives of their students."
—Solomon Ortiz

"I have come to believe that a great teacher is a great artist and that there are as few as there are any other great artists. Teaching might even be the greatest of the arts since the medium is the human mind and spirit."
—John Steinbeck

"I touch the future. I teach."

—Christa McAuliffe

"I cannot emphasize enough the importance of a good teacher."

– Temple Grandin

"I am indebted to my father for living, but to my teacher for living well."
-Alexander the Great

"Everybody's a teacher if you listen."

–Doris Roberts

> "The whole art of teaching is only the art of awakening the natural curiosity of young minds for the purpose of satisfying it afterwards."
> –Anatole France

"I'm lucky I had some teachers who saw something in me."

-Ann Bancroft

> "Only one person in a million becomes enlightened without a teacher's help."
>
> —Bodhidharma

"The true teacher defends his pupils against his own personal influence. He inspires self-trust. He guides their eyes from himself to the spirit that quickens him." —Amos Bronson Alcott

"A teacher is a person who never says anything once."

–Howard Nemerov